Making the Grade

Martial Arts Memoirs

Martin Cousins

Order this book online at www.trafford.com
or email orders@trafford.com

Most Trafford titles are also available at major online book retailers.

Printed in the United States of America.

ISBN: 978-1-4269-9442-5 (sc)

Trafford rev. 08/30/2011

 www.trafford.com

North America & international
toll-free: 1 888 232 4444 (USA & Canada)
phone: 250 383 6864 ♦ fax: 812 355 4082

Dedication

To my lovely wife, Anne, who has stood by my side for so long, who is my strength and who keeps me going when times get hard.

She has made me what I am today.

My friend, my love, my inspiration.

Acknowledgements

Many people have inspired my life in Kenpo and have also inspired this book. While there are many others too numerous to mention, I would like to thank the following in particular.

- Tommy Jordan
- Dave Quinn
- Richie Mahony
- Tommy Kane
- Niall McGowan
- Sean Smith
- Elizabeth Kelly
- Eamon Kelly
- The family of the late Michael Watson

Contents

List of Illustrations

CHAPTER 1

The Man from America

Karate in Ireland is fortunate in having as its founding father one of the greatest of the Kenpo Grandmasters, John McSweeney.

John McSweeney was born in Brooklyn, New York. His father was an attorney and his mother was a school teacher. John was raised in a tough city neighbourhood, where he may have discovered the need to fight in self-defence. He learnt Judo when he was young, and his interest in martial arts continued while he was in the army. He was a very powerful man, five foot ten inches tall and weighing 190-200 lbs. He trained with some of the best in the field of martial arts, including Jimmy Woo and James Lee. He was one of the first in a group of Americans that Grandmaster Ed Parker, who brought the art of Chinese Kenpo to the United States, taught in Los Angeles.

Figure 1. John McSweeney

John McSweeney and his wife both had Irish roots; John's mother came from County Cork and his father came from County Kerry and John's wife's family came from County Clare. So when John McSweeney came from America to Ireland in 1963, in some ways it was a homecoming.

John McSweeney was also a very intelligent man. He had two reasons for coming to Ireland. He wanted to take a Master's degree in economic geography from Trinity College, Dublin. He also wanted to introduce Kenpo Karate to Ireland and Europe.

John had been granted his black belt by Ed Parker in September 1962. Now he was anxious to pass on his knowledge.

Figure 2. John McSweeney and Tommy Jordan, c.1983

John lost no time in renting premises in 40 Upper Fitzwilliam St. and founding the Irish Karate Association. He advertised in the press and, on the 26th of February 1963, Kenpo Karate classes started for the first time ever in Europe. He was an exceptional fighter and teacher who concentrated mostly on the self-defence aspects of karate. He believed in fast, powerful and effective strikes to vulnerable areas. He was a true believer in teaching practical techniques for street fighting.

John's first student was Tommy Jordan who already had an interest in martial arts, and had attended demonstrations in Judo at the National Stadium. Tommy was fortunate to be working less than 100 metres away from the club as a dental technician, and joined immediately. All the students had to be over 18 and only men took part. The first women to participate in Kenpo were much later in the Rathgar Kenpo club.

There were other students as well who had had experience in different areas of fighting, but who also wanted to benefit from John McSweeney's experience. Often they tried to test him. Tommy Jordan tells the story of one fighter from a wrestling background who came to the club and had a private lesson with him. Suddenly he asked 'What would you do against this, John?' He then gave John a very strong bear hug. That was no problem to the Kenpo instructor who gave the wrestler a reverse back fist to the temple. The wrestler sank to the floor, where he was left to recover.

Other people would arrive drunk at the club with enough dutch courage to want to challenge the instructor. John McSweeney dealt with them easily. He would approach them and demonstrate what he was teaching. He would then throw a karate chop to their temple or voice box and they would quickly leave.

In September 1963, the Irish Karate Association got national coverage on the Irish national television station, RTE. The Late Late Show, hosted by Gay Byrne, was the most popular and prestigious television show in Ireland. John McSweeney did some board breaking and he and Tommy Jordan demonstrated some self-defence techniques. This really impressed the audience and increased the membership of the club.

Figure 3. Tommy Jordan and John McSweeney practising techniques

Unfortunately Ireland in the 1960s was not prosperous. A combination of the poor economic future in Ireland and the sunnier weather in America enticed John McSweeney back to the United States at the end of 1964. He was anxious that all the good work that he had done in setting up the Irish Karate Association would not be wasted. He selected four of his best students, Tommy Jordan, James (Jimmy) Rice, John Conway and Maurice Mahon and made them train extra hard, in the hope that he could recommend them for black belts to Ed Parker, and so ensure the future of Kenpo Karate in Ireland. They all succeeded in this and Tommy Jordan was the first person to receive black belt certification from Ed Parker, both in Ireland and Europe, in February 1965. He proudly hung the certificate on the wall in Fitzwilliam Street.

Figure 4. Tommy Jordan, John Conway and Jimmy Rice

Tommy Jordan and Maurice Mahon bought the good will of the club in Fitzwilliam St. from John McSweeney and continued to teach there.

Figure 5. Irish Kenpo students, Fitzwilliam Club, Baggot St., 1964

Other Irish Kenpo students left, as many Irish did, for England and took their new Kenpo skills with them. Ronnie Gurey, although he was a white belt, started to teach students in Swindon. His students included Phil Hegarty, Pete Presswell, and Martin Sleeman. Phil Hegarty in his turn founded the Kenpo Karate club in Walcot Common, and invited some of the Irish Kenpo instructors to come over and teach. These included Jimmy Rice, one of the original Irish black belts, and Brendan Walsh as well as Tommy Jordan. Phil Hegarty put Tommy Jordan in touch with Len Palmer, the secretary of the All Britain Karate-Do Association with a view to joining the European Karate Union.

Figure 6. John McSweeney and Jimmy Rice, 1983

Figure 7. Tommy Jordan and John McSweeney, 1983

John McSweeney continued teaching Kenpo in America, and was regarded as one of Ed Parker's finest Grandmasters. He was remembered and respected by his Irish students. He returned to Dublin in 1983 and was presented with a trophy by Tommy Jordan. He died in 2002.

CHAPTER 2

Tommy Jordan

Figure 8. Tommy Jordan

Dun Laoghaire Kenpo Karate has a proud lineage. It was started by Tommy Jordan, a pupil of John McSweeney, who was himself one of the first pupils of Ed Parker. The history of Karate in Dun Laoghaire, and indeed Ireland, owes a great debt to Tommy Jordan. As John McSweeney's first pupil in February 1963, he had both huge aptitude and great enthusiasm for martial arts. He was so enthusiastic that John gave him the keys to the club so that he could arrive early and train for an hour before each class. It was not unusual for Tommy to train for four or five hours every night. He would position himself on the left side of John McSweeney and imitate all of his techniques, sometimes doing it so well that John McSweeney would think that he had studied the techniques before.

Figure 9. Tommy Jordan and Jimmy Rice demonstrating a self-defence move, 1964

Tommy was just over six foot tall, and light for his height, weighing about 140 lbs. at that time. Some of the weight lifters and wrestlers at the club thought that they could intimidate him by their bulk. However, Tommy showed his determination in two ways.

Firstly, he trained extremely hard, concentrating on stretching and kicking techniques. He could throw very high kicks fast and easily, and from this he developed a lot of very skilful combination moves.

Secondly he consulted a friend who was a doctor on how the body's nervous system worked, and borrowed some books from him. These showed him exactly the best places to strike, especially the radial, median and ulna nerves on the arm. To ensure maximum impact, and taking advantage of his naturally tough bone structure, he developed the hardness of his knuckles.

This quickly discouraged any attempts by weight lifters to intimidate Tommy!

Figure 10. Tommy Jordan

Left: Self-defence demonstration, Mansion House, 1980
Right: Weapons form demonstration

Kenpo Karate in Ireland developed in different ways. In this it echoed the development in Kenpo worldwide. When John McSweeney first came to Ireland, he brought with him the original Kenpo styles as taught by Grandmaster Ed Parker. This is what he taught Tommy Jordan and the other members of the first Kenpo Karate club in Ireland in Fitzwilliam Street.

However, Ed Parker himself decided to change the style in which he taught Kenpo Karate. This has lead to a situation in Ireland where two different types of Karate were taught; Ed Parker's old system which he had taught to John McSweeney and which McSweeney had taught in the first Irish Kenpo club, and the new style which Ed Parker promoted from the mid seventies on.

The new style had two main problems. While Ed Parker could demonstrate it perfectly, the new terminology was difficult to understand and the people he taught found it hard to teach. Some of the moves were so complicated that they were not practical. Kenpo Karate has always been about street fighting and self-defence and these moves would not have been any usc in these situations.

With the new style also came a system of franchises. John Conway wanted the I.K.A. to become involved but it would have cost the association a large sum of money every year from all the clubs to pay the club fees, grading fees instructors fees and association fees. The I.K.A. did not believe that it would get enough benefit from spending so much money. Instead Tommy Jordan continued to streamline and develop the original system that he had been taught by John McSweeney.

Figure 11. Peter Coyle, John Conway and Tommy Jordan, Los Angeles, 1983

John Conway and Jimmy Rice decided to teach the new style of Kenpo professionally. John Conway taught in the Kenpo Karate club in Baggot St. but eventually emigrated to America in Los Angeles. Jimmy Rice and two of his students kept the two schools going.

The franchise system eventually lead to the I.K.A. being refused the right to use the I.K.K.A name or crest. The I.K.K.A had registered the name Kenpo Karate and crest in Ireland and threatened legal action against any person or club not associated with it who used them. On September 30th 1982, Rainer Schulte who claimed to represent Ed Parker in Europe wrote to the I.KA. to say that it had lost its representation on the I.K.K.A., on account of its failure to uphold Ed Parker's standards of proficiency. However Mr. Schulte had never seen Tommy Jordan teaching or training, so it is hard to escape the conclusion that other factors, such as the franchise fee were at work.

Tommy Jordan continued to teach at the Rathgar Kenpo Studios, the headquarters of the I.KA. This club had been started and built up by Peter Coyle and Dave Quinn. Peter Coyle is still president there and also president of the National Body for Karate in Ireland (O.N.A.K.A.I.) which Tommy Jordan helped to found in 1978.

Figure 12. Tommy Jordan gains his 6th Dan

Tommy Jordan is a man of immense skill but great modesty. He believes that grades have to be earned. On one occasion he was sent a 7th degree black Dan belt by John McSweeney, but refused to wear it because he did not consider himself to be worthy enough. He was eventually awarded his 7th Dan and a lifetime achievement award by his peers.

Tommy Jordan is always proud that he had been taught by John McSweeney. He is determined to keep up the high standard of Kenpo that he had been taught, and has little respect for those who claim to have a high standard and who then cannot demonstrate proficiency.

Figure 13. Tommy Jordan receives an award for 21 years in Karate from Peter Coyle

CHAPTER 3

Dun Laoghaire - The Early Days

Figure 14. Site of Old Judo Club, Salthill, Dun Laoghaire

I started martial arts in the 1960s, when my father brought my brother and me to the Judo classes that were held in the tennis club beside Salthill train station in Dun Laoghaire.

Figure 15. My Father, Bert Cousins, and I

Even after I stopped Judo, and started playing football instead, I kept an interest in Karate. I first saw a demonstration of Kenpo at a Christmas party for the St. John Bosco youth club held in Blackrock College.

Figure 16. Martial arts venues, 1960s and 1970s

Left: St. John Bosco Youth Club
Right: Adelaide Road, Dun Laoghaire

Tommy Jordan started Kenpo classes in the 1960s in premises on Adelaide Road in Dun Laoghaire.

Figure 17. Tommy Jordan and Eamon Nolan sparring, Adelaide Road, c. 1970

His early students included Peter Coyle, Paul Rogers, Jimmy Boylan, Dave Quinn, Eamon Nolan, Ronan Daly, Tommy Kane, Brian Keegan, Roy Whiston and many others. By the time I joined the classes he had moved to the Workman's Club on Library Road.

Figure 18. Workman's Club, Dun Laoghaire

The club house was at the rear of the Workman's club and had no facilities, not even showers. At one point in the late 1980s I remember that the rent was not paid and the electricity was cut off. We ended up training by candlelight.

Figure 19. Tommy Jordan at the Dun Laoghaire Workman's Club

Figure 20. Tommy Kane, Roy Whiston and Brian Keegan

Demonstration of a two man self-defence technique, Adelaide Rd. Dun Laoghaire, c.1969

Despite this, a lot of people from Dun Laoghaire started Kenpo; some lasted for a week while others remained in the club for years. Tommy's reputation was such that students came not only from Dun Laoghaire, but also from as far away as Dublin city centre, Rathgar, Rathmines and Bray.

Figure 21. Tommy Kane and Brian Keegan

I discovered that Tommy's karate classes were only two minutes from my house and decided to join the club in 1971-1972. Tommy was wearing a white suit that night with a crest on it. I had not realised that Kenpo was one of many different styles of martial arts. Eventually many different styles of karate came to Ireland. Kenpo Karate was like street fighting; you could use techniques such as open hand strikes, groin kicks, elbows and grabs.

Figure 22. Dun Laoghaire Kenpo Karate Club, Workman's Club, Dun Laoghaire, 1972

Left to Right:
Back Row: Tommy Jordan, Pat Murtagh, Paul Rogers
Front Row: Eamon Nolan, Peter Coyle, Jimmy Boylan, Dave Quinn

Figure 23. Tommy Jordan and student, c. 1969, Dun Laoghaire

Michael (Mick) Watson, Richie Mahony, Tommy Lawlor and I joined at the same time. We all lived close to the club and were able to train together regularly.

Figure 24. Early days in Dun Laoghaire and Rathgar

Clockwise:
Martin Cousins sparring with Richie Mahony
Tommy Lawlor and Dave Quinn, 1972
Mick Watson and Martin Cousins, 1977
Dave Quinn sparring, 1972

Other students who were already there were Jimmy Boylan, a great friend of Tommy Jordan, Peter Coyle, David Quinn, Paul Rogers, Ronan Daly and Eamon Nolan, who would all become black belts. Jimmy Boylan left soon after I joined to start training in Ballybough, at North Strand in Dublin, where Tommy Jordan also acted as an instructor.

Tommy Jordan was completely dedicated to the club. Despite having to travel in all weathers on his Heinkel scooter from North Strand, he was never late. He was motivated by a love of Kenpo, rather than by financial rewards

Tommy, like John McSweeney emphasised self-defence techniques. He made his pupils work hard, putting great emphasis on blocks, strikes, speed and focus. In those days, the grading system consisted of two white belts and three brown belts. The first white belt had two brown stripes, one on each side of the belt. The syllabus contained 80 defence techniques, blocking form, form one and sparring for the first tip grade. Sparring was much tougher in those days. It was called wall to wall sparring and this meant that you literally got knocked from wall to wall.

I took my first test after a year and had to wait a week for the result. I failed because I had hesitated on some of the self-defence techniques. I can't remember if I was very disappointed, but it taught me never to give up.

Figure 25. Grading for my 2nd tip with Dave Quinn, 1973

The grading system was difficult and it was hard to gain a black belt. It usually took over five years of hard work. There were very few competitions in those days, since clubs were few and far between. This meant that most of my early years were spent training for grades.

The late Mick Watson, Richie Mahony and Tommy Lawlor and I helped one another to prepare for grades. We frequently trained outside club hours, sometimes in my house and sometimes in Tommy Lawlor's house.

Figure 26. Practising in Dun Laoghaire

Clockwise:
Tommy Lawlor and Martin Cousins
Tony Reynolds and Martin Cousins training, 1975
Paul Rogers and Pat Murtagh sparring, Dun Laoghaire, 1972

Paul Rogers often opened the club at weekends to give us extra classes on Saturday afternoons and Sunday mornings when people were preparing for the grades.

Paul, or Rog, as most people called him, was extremely generous with his encouragement and time, and I owe him a great deal. He later went to America and now lives in Chicago.

The first black belt grading I saw was that of Eamon Nolan in 1974. Eamon was very good at demonstrating self-defence, and was always great to watch. He could also motivate students to train hard, even if he he stood over you and grinned while you worked!

Figure 27. Eamon Nolan and Paul Rogers

In 1974 Dave Quinn opened a club in Rathgar. The premises belonged to his relations and Dave lived near Rathgar himself, so Tommy Jordan went out there to teach classes and help Dave to establish Kenpo in that part of Dublin. Peter Coyle, Paul Rogers, Richie Mahony, Mick Watson, and I all followed Tommy to Rathgar. Ronan Daly was left in charge of Dun Laoghaire.

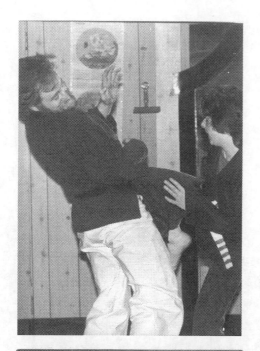

Figure 28. Scenes from Rathgar Studio

Clockwise:
Dave Quinn and Irene Oglesby,
Tommy Jordan and Dave Quinn
Tommy Jordan and Richie Mahony,
Mick Watson and Richie Mahony

In 1975 three more students graded to black belt. These were Ronan Daly, Paul Rogers and Dave Quinn. Ronan liked to train hard in all types of weather. Whether it was hail, rain or snow, we would train in the back yard with combinations, kicks, punches and drills. The students would do on a regular basis 1000 kicks, 1000 punches and 1000 push-ups in a night's training. When Ronan started weight-training, he made his own weights with concrete, and would not appreciate anybody helping him out if the weights looked too heavy.

Figure 29. Ronan Daly

Left: Ronan Daly practising
Right: Ronan Daly and Eamon Nolan, 1972

Ronan's training saved his life on one occasion at least. He fell down a glacier in Canada and was seriously frostbitten and hurt. It was his physical strength, gained from his martial arts training, that enabled him to survive.

Ronan concentrated hard when he trained. He was a fierce fighter and a very strong instructor. I ended up with a busted lip on more than one occasion.

In 1976 Peter Coyle graded to black belt. He was always very strong, and practising self-defence with Peter was not for the faint-hearted. His blocks were very powerful and you were left with very sore arms the next day. Peter was always in great shape. I didn't realize it at that time but he must have being weight training from when he was young.

Figure 30. Tommy Jordan and Peter Coyle

Back in Dun Laoghaire, kick boxing was introduced and the club eventually became a kick boxing club. Body armour and head gear were used as it was very easy for someone to be knocked out.

Figure 31. Martin Cousins doing a roundhouse kick against John Hunter from Sallynoggin, 1977

Karate in Dun Laoghaire provided a great way to get fit, learn self-defence and make good friends. I will always be grateful to those who encouraged me and helped me start training in martial arts.

CHAPTER 4

Competition at Home

The Irish Karate Association (I.K.A.) was founded by John McSweeney in 1963. In 1968 an umbrella organisation, the All Ireland Karate Federation (A.I.K.F.) was founded, which included the I.K.A and the Shotokan and Wadu Ryu karate clubs which were in Dublin and the Northern Ireland. This meant that competitions could be held in Ireland. The first ever competition took place in 1968 in Moran's Hotel in Gardiner Street. Unfortunately the A.I.K.F. did not last long because Tatsu Susuki, who was the senior Wadu Ryu instructor did not want the clubs in Northern Ireland to be associated with clubs in the Republic of Ireland.

In 1972 I had my first competition. I was on a five man team which Tommy Jordan used to demonstrate Kenpo Karate at a school in Co. Dublin.

Figure 32. Karate Competition, Dublin, 1972

Martin Cousins first competition fight, with Tommy Jordan refereeing

Figure 33. Demonstrations

Left: Dave Quinn and Martin Cousins demonstrating sparring
Top right: Martin Cousins demonstrating breaking
Bottom right: Dave Quinn and Martin Cousins demonstrating sparring

Five students, all white belts, John Kilkenny, Pat Murtagh, Mick Watson, Alan Shortall and I took part in a team event for junior grades. Dun Laoghaire won. John Kilkenny was the team captain and received a trophy and the rest of the team received medals. I still have this medal in my possession.

Alan Shortall eventually emigrated from Ireland to Australia.

This was the competition that really gave me my first taste for competitive fighting, which I still enjoy.

Figure 34. 1972 Competition

Top: Left to Right: John Kilkenny, Pat Murtagh, Mick Watson, Martin Cousins and Alan Shortall
Bottom Right: Left to Right Back Row: Dave Quinn, Eamon Nolan, Jimmy Rice, Tommy Jordan, Eugene Healy: Front
Row: Peter Coyle, Paul Rogers, Jimmy Boylan, Alan Shortall
Bottom Left: Peter Coyle, Paul Rogers and Jimmy Boylan

The senior grades took part in an open weight division. Most of the students were brown belts. Paul Rogers from Dun Laoghaire Kenpo club won, Jimmy Boylan was second and Peter Coyle was third.

Tommy and the senior grades gave a demonstration of self-defence forms and breaking to a packed hall.

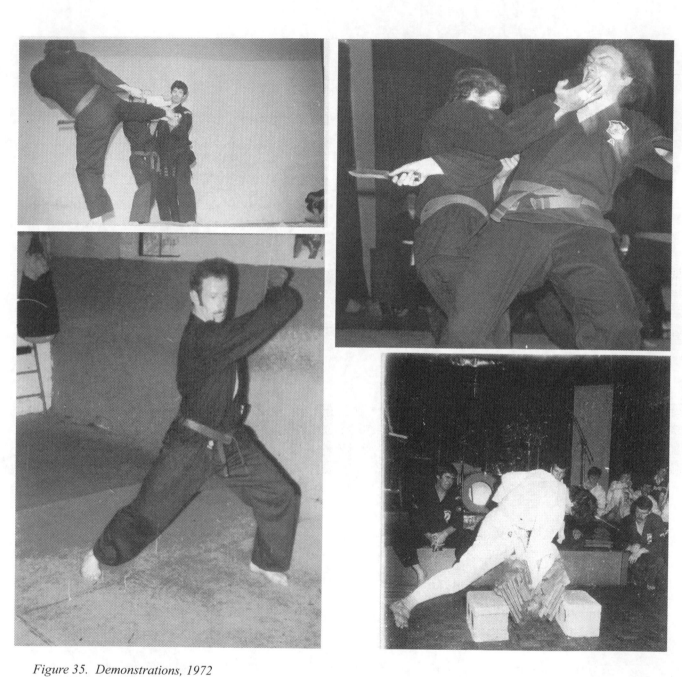

Figure 35. Demonstrations, 1972

Clockwise:
Paul Rogers demonstrates breaking
Eamon Nolan and Paul Rogers demonstrate a self-defence technique against a knife attack, 1972
Rory Comerford demonstrates breaking
Peter Coyle demonstrates forms

In 1974, Ed Parker himself came to Dublin with some other Kenpo Karate experts, and held some classes and did some demonstrations in the Burlington Hotel. They included Tom Kelly, who was known as 'Big Bear' Kelly and was a member of the American team that fought in Europe in the 1970s.

Figure 36. Visit of Ed Parker to Dublin, 1974

Clockwise:
Ed Parker and Peter Coyle
Ed Parker and Jimmy Boylan
Tommy Jordan, Jimmy Rice, Tom Kelly and George Quinones

You had to be at least a brown belt to take Ed Parkers's class. Unfortunately, I was only a white belt at the time, but I did get to go with my wife, Anne, to the dinner dance at the Burlington, where there was a demonstration.

Tommy organised other demonstrations, sometimes in the open air.

Figure 37. Demonstration in Dublin, 1977

Demonstrations were a great way to get interest in Kenpo Karate. However, they could be dangerous. In later years one student, Derek McKeever ended up with a knife in his foot during a demonstration. Once I dislocated my shoulder when Anne, my wife, demonstrated a self-defence technique against a muggers grab at Cabinteely school.

Ronan Daly liked sparring and some years later introduced semi-contact points fighting in Dun Laoghaire

He had being training with Peter Spanton, one of England's top fighters, in Higashi karate. He had seen a new type of competitive fighting, points sparring. He brought Peter over to the club to give seminars in the early 80s.

Figure 38. Peter Spanton

Left: Peter Spanton and Martin Cousins, Madrid 1980
Right: Tommy Lawlor, Mick Watson and Peter Spanton, Dublin

The rules were different. There were three points for a high kick, spinning kick or jump kick and two points for a body kick. Hand and feet combinations and sweeps got three points. Straight forward strikes received one point. Since each fight lasted three minutes, you could score a lot of points.

It was much harder to score in traditional karate fights. You received half a point for straight punch, back-knuckle and low kicks and a full point for high kicks and sweeps. However, the strikes had to be well executed and it was very hard to score at times. The first fighter to score six points was the winner.

Dave Quinn and Peter Coyle were keen on competitive karate. The Irish Karate championships had just become a yearly event, and Dave and Peter started extra classes. These classes were held purely to train for competitions. This meant that we were better trained for competitive fighting and one step ahead of the opposition.

Figure 39. Dave Quinn and Paul Rogers, 1973

In 1977 we entered a competition in Fitzwilliam club in Baggot street, Dublin. The club was run by John Conway and Jimmy Rice, who were teaching full time.

The Fitzwilliam club facilities were magnificent. The club was well laid out; the fighting area had a red carpet. There were spacious dressing rooms and shower facilities. It was a huge contrast to our facilities in Dun Laoghaire.

Figure 40. Fitzwilliam Club, Baggot St., 1977
Left to Right: Richie Mahony, Mick Watson and Martin Cousins

Richie, Mick, Tommy Lawlor and I were all brown belts then and were very competitive. There was very few competitions in those days. If you were beaten in a tournament it could be six months before the next one.

You met all sorts of people in Kenpo competitions. In one tournament in Baggot street, I was fighting a student whom I had never met before. I beat him completely and even knocked him down a few times. I felt great until after the tournament was over and we were changing in the dressing room. I saw him put on a clerical collar and realised that he was a priest. Times were different in those days, and assaulting a priest would have been considered a serious matter, even if he had gone into the competition voluntarily. If I had told my mother I had hit a priest, I would have being thrown out of the house. I never met the priest again but I expect he forgave me.

In another tournament in Baggot street, all the participants were getting ready to fight when a person came in off the street. He was wearing a karate suit and he registered to fight. As he was limbering up, he started to imitate Bruce Lee by doing all the cat calls.

'Jesus, this one must be good', one student nervously said. Yet when it came to his turn to fight, he didn't last a minute. As he walked off the floor, near the door he dropped down into a push-up position and rattled off thirty push-ups. He then got up, walked out the of door, and was never see again.

Sometimes celebrities were asked to present medals at the competitions. I remember one Sunday morning after a tournament in Fitzwilliam club being presented with a medal by Brendan Grace the well-known Dublin comedian.

In 1978 Mick Watson tested for black belt and in 1979 Richie Mahony also graded to black belt.

I was training hard in 1979 but one night in Rathgar, while training I fell to the floor with back pain. Little did I know the problem would haunt me till the present day.

Figure 41. Trophy Winners

Left: Rathgar Team, 1980s Richie Mahony, Peter Coyle, Mick Watson, Dave Quinn and Paul Rogers
Right: Richie Mahony with some of his trophies

I took some time off and after a few weeks decided to train again in Dun Laoghaire under Ronan Daly. The club was still producing good students and there were some great fighters coming up. These included Mel Curry, Frank Johnson, Liam Whelan, Henry O'Gorman, and many more. Tommy Lawlor was still training at the club and was a great help when I trained for my black belt, as were Mel and all the other students. I was all set for my grade in December 1979, but a mix up in dates with Tommy Jordan delayed it until January 1980.

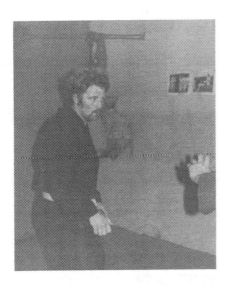

Figure 42. Henry O'Gorman and Frank Johnson

The first O.N.A.K.A.I. national championships were held in 1980 in the national stadium.

I fought on the Rathgar team with Richie and Mick. However, we did better in the individual events than in the team events. Mel Curry won his first national championship title for Dun Laoghaire and I reached the final in the heavyweight division, only to lose to Paul Duffy who practised Shotokan karate.

Figure 43. O.N.A.K.A.I. Heavyweight Final, Martin Cousins and Paul Duffy, 1980

In 1983 I won the I.K.A championships and was runner up again in the O.N.A.K.A.I. heavy weight final, being beaten once more by Paul Duffy. The team were second in the team event.

Figure 44. Sparring at the O.N.A.K.A.I. finals, 1980s

Figure 45. I.K.A.Championships

Clockwise:
Ballybrack Workman's Club, I.K.A. runners-up, 1983 Back Row: John Kirwan, Martin Cousins, Jim Maguire Front
Row: Terry Cousins, Liam Farrelly, Peter Dillon
Martin Cousins I.K.A. champion, 1983
I.K.A. Championships 1985, Dick Comerford, Richie Mahony, Brian O'Toole and Martin Cousins
Mick Watson fighting at the I.K.A. Championships

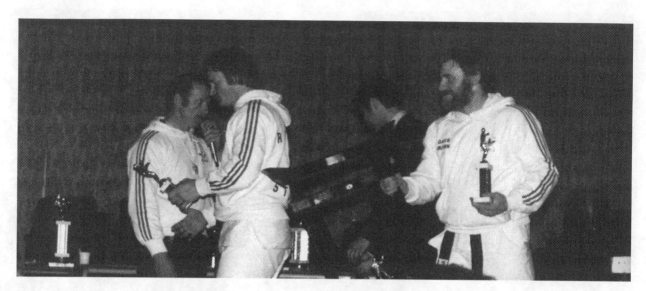

Figure 46. I.K.A. Championships, 1985, Team Winners
Left to Right: Peter Coyle, Richie Mahony, Tommy Jordan and Dave Quinn

In 1986 the Dublin invitational karate tournament was held and Mick Byrne took first place in the under 65 kilo division. I fought for Rathgar in the team event and we were beaten in the final. I reached the final of the individual heavy weight division but lost out again.

Figure 47. Mick Byrne and Martin Cousins, O.N.A.K.A.I. championship medallists

Competition at home was a great way to sharpen our skills as well as meet other fighters and learn from their techniques. In addition, it allowed me to move to the next stage of my life in martial arts, representing Ireland.

CHAPTER 5

International Competition

The first international Karate competition in which Ireland took part was in 1966. The Irish Karate Association entered two Karate competitions in America, one in New York and the other in Rhode Island. The team were Tommy Jordan, Jim Clark, Jimmy Rice and John Conway. The team trained in John McSweeney's club with Eddie Quinones, a brother of George Quinones and another student, Bobby Herbts. The Irish lads won all their fights in America.

The first Irish team to enter the European Karate Unions (E.K.U.) championships were Tommy Jordan, Mick Molloy, Jimmy Rice, Wally Pidgeon, Jim Pritchard, Mervyn Street, Des Irwin and Gerard Keenan. They fought at Crystal Palace in London.

Ireland was a signatory at the formation of the World Union of Karate Organisations (W.U.K.O) in Paris. The first president was Jack Delcourt who was very supportive of Ireland's involvement. The I.K.A. continued to represent Ireland in the E.K.U. and the W.U.K.O. championships for many years. The I.K.A. introduced new moves in the championships, including back-knuckles, spinning heel kicks and blade kicks. They promoted Kenpo Karate as competitors and delegates. At this early point there were no other Kenpo Karate clubs involved at the championships, although there were other Kenpo clubs in Germany and Jersey.

Paul Rogers was the first fighter in Ireland to win a European fight and it was his encouragement over the years that helped me to eventually win a place on the national squad. However, the first person who ever thought that I would represent Ireland was Eamon Nolan. When I was training as a white belt in a large class of students I tried a high kick and landed on my back side. Everyone laughed, but Eamon stopped the class and told them that I would fight for Ireland one day.

In 1978 I was selected to represent Ireland, along with Peter Coyle, Mick Watson, Dave Quinn and Hugh Harmony, at the European Championships in Geneva, Switzerland. Hugh Harmony was a real Dubliner and had a strong Dublin accent. I have sadly never met Hugh since. Richie Mahony just missed out on selection. Tommy Jordan and Jim Clark also travelled as officials. Jim Clark had being doing a lot of work in the background with the I.K.A and was awarded an honorary black belt some years later by all the black belts under Tommy Jordan. He eventually opened his own club.

Figure 48. Irish Team, Geneva 1978, training in Baggot St.

Left to Right: Jim Clark, Hugh Harmony, Martin Cousins, Dave Quinn, Mick Watson and Peter Coyle

I remember all the teams, except the Irish team, wearing brand new tracksuits at the opening ceremony. The Irish national team had to wear karate suits as we could not afford a team outfit. It was one of many embarrassing moments over the years that we endured on the national team.

Figure 49. Irish team, Geneva 1978, in our karate suits

Left to Right: Martin Cousins, Dave Quinn, Peter Coyle, Hugh Harmony and Mick Watson

Mick and I decided to see Geneva and left the stadium. After a while we lost our way. I will never forget Mick trying to explain to the locals that we were lost and needed help to find the stadium. Nobody Mick talked to could understand his attempts to talk the local language!

Unfortunately we did not win the European championships. When they were over, we were all depressed. We returned to the hotel and, in a typically Irish fashion, drowned our sorrows by making full use of the duty free we had bought on our way out, and the cold drinks machine and ice-maker in the hotel. When I got back to Ireland I made a promise never to drink at a tournament again. That team was the last full Kenpo team to be selected for the national team. The Official National Amateur Karate Association of Ireland (O.N.A.K.A.I.) was formed, bringing most of the different karate styles together at that time. Tommy Jordan, Peter Coyle and John Conway represented Kenpo. Tommy McGrain, chief instructor of the Irish region of the K.U.G.B represented Shotokan karate and Iwasaki chief instructor for all Ireland Karate-Do, also sat on the committee.

Figure 50. O.N.A.K.A.I. Founders, 1978

Squad training started soon after our return from the championships in Geneva. At stake was a place on the Irish team to compete in Madrid in the world championships in November. The training sessions were held in Gardiner Street in Dublin at the headquarters of Wado Ki.

I remember their was no love loss between the different styles and fighting was tough. Kenpo at that time was frowned upon, especially by the Japanese, who regarded it as a bastard style because it originated in China.

Mick Watson, Richie Mahony, the Iwasaki team coach Derek Desmond, Francis Nangle, Robert McGrath, Michael Guilfoyle and I were in the O.N.A.K.A.I. team that represented Ireland at the World Union of Karate Organizations (W.U.K.O.) world championships in Madrid, Spain in November 1980.

Figure 51. O.N.A.K.A.I. Irish team, 1980

In the finals of the men's individuals open weight category, Derek Desmond took 5th place and in the Kata Michael Guilfoyle took 7th in his section. A total of 53 countries participated. This was the largest ever attendance at the W.U.K.O world championships since the first one in Tokyo in 1969, at which 33 countries participated.

Figure 52. Madrid 1980

Clockwise:
Top left: Mick Watson and Martin Cousins
Top right: Mick Watson
Bottom: Sparring

I will never forget the World Championships in Madrid. From the time we got to the hotel, we started training. We trained for seven hours a day for three days. We started with a three mile run and then trained in the local park for several hours, finishing off with push-ups on our knuckles in the gravel. After dinner, we were told to train again, and had to set off on another three mile run.

The night before the World Championship started, we trained in the basement of the hotel. There was no ventilation and, worst still, there was carpet on the floor. After five minutes we all had blisters.

Later that night in my room I cut the blisters on my feet open with a blade, as I could not walk. We fought Japan in the first round, but didn't fare well.

Kick boxing was only starting in Ireland. We were told we could only do traditional fighting, as we were not allowed to join another organization. This seemed strange as we met the Australian national team and they were all practising kick boxing.

However, it was not all bad news. We got to meet some great fighters including the World Champion, Tokey Hill.

Figure 53. World Champion Tokey Hill and Martin Cousins, Madrid 1980

In May 1981, I was selected again to fight for Ireland at the European Karate Championships in Venice, Italy. Dave Quinn and Peter Coyle from Kenpo had made the team as well.

Figure 54. Venice, 1981

Left: Peter Coyle, Martin Cousins and Dave Quinn
Right: Derek Desmond, Robert McGrath, Dave Quinn and Martin Cousins

Dave received a bad head injury while trying to board a boat. The swell in the lagoon tilted the boat and Dave caught his head on the doorway. He was lucky that he did not fall between the boat and the pier.

He was taken by boat launch to hospital. It was the gloomiest and most medieval-looking building I have ever seen. All the team returned the next day to see Dave. It was not unusual for the competitors to wear their karate uniform outside the sports stadium with a tracksuit top over their suit; this was what Dave had been wearing. When we saw Dave, still in his blood splattered karate suit with a stocking bandage over his head, we were all shocked.

Dave begged us to get his clothes, so we did and took Dave out of a side door and back to the hotel.

We delayed our flight home by a day to give Dave a chance to recover. The hotel management team promised to organise this. However, when we arrived at the airport the next day, we could not get our flight home, and we ended up flying home via Brussels and an over-night stay in London.

In May 1982 I made the Irish team again for the European Karate Championships in Gothenburg, Sweden. Richie Mahony and Dave Quinn had made the team as well. Peter Coyle was now the coach.

Figure 55. Sweden 1982

Clockwise:
Irish Team
Richie Mahony and Martin Cousins
Lining out with Jeff Thompson
Richie Mahony sparring

In the team event we fought England and I lined up against Jeff Thompson who was a world champion. I remember hitting Jeff with a straight kick to the body, but his arms were so long he punched over my kick and hit me in the sternum and I nearly bit my gum shield in half.

I remember Gothenburg was a lovely clean city.

In May 1983 I made the Irish team again. It was the European Karate Championships in Madrid. Peter was the coach once more. This time a young fighter from Rathgar, Rory Comerford, made the team. It was unusual because Rory was not yet a brown belt but he was an exceptional fighter. He went on to win many national titles. I was to fight Rory many times in the I.K.A championships.

Figure 56. Madrid 1983

Left: Irish Team, Madrid,1983
Right: Martin Cousins and Rory Comerford relaxing

In the same year O.N.A.K.A.I. decided to send a team to the E.K.U championships in Munich, Germany. Another karate group who opposed O.N.A.K.A.I. sent a team, so two Irish teams travelled. O.N.A.K.A.I. had not got a strong representation in the E.K.U, and lost out at the congress meeting before the championships started. It was the only time we lost out to another Irish team. Our team supported the other Irish team from the stands in the stadium.

Figure 57. Germany 1984

Left: Irish Team, Peter Coyle, Alan Campbell, Jim Boot, Martin Cousins, Larry Hand, Ray Payne, Eamon Elliot
Right: Peter Coyle, Jim Boot, Martin Cousins

The grand slam was held in Scotland in 1984. Richie Mahony and I made the team. This time the Irish team was fortunate, taking second in the team event. I was injured in the semi-final and ended up in hospital, missing the final.

Figure 58. Grand Slam, Scotland, 1984

Figure 59. With my goddaughter, Lia, 1984

Figure 60. Grand slams and other tournaments

Clockwise:

Leading out the Irish Team, Dublin, 1981
Paul Jordan, Tommy Jordan and Martin Cousins, Scotland, 1984
Local tournament winners, Oban, Scotland,1984
Martin Cousins with the runner up team trophy, Scotland, 1984

In 1997 we entered a joint team from Rathgar and Deansgrange for the European Kenpo Karate Championships.

Figure 61. Squad training, 1997

Figure 62. European Kenpo Championships, Dublin, 1997

I was working hard with Dave Ryan, who was one of Tommy Jordan's black belts to push the I.K.A into more competitions. I ended up winning two medals at the European championships, but I would have preferred it if my students had won.

Figure 63. European Kenpo Championships, Dublin, 1997
Left to Right: Dave Ryan, Derek McKeever and Martin Cousins

Dave Ryan, Tony Devine, Kevin Kane, Ross Cowap, Niall McGowan and Derek McKeever all fought very well but missed out on the medals.

In 2000 we travelled to France and Switzerland with two full-contact fighters, Owen Dempsey and Jonathan Lewins, and with three other fighters from Ireland, Jimmy Upton, Padraig Murphy and Darren Duncan. The event was the post Tenebras cup, and the team did well, winning their fights.

Figure 64. Post Tenebras Cup 2000

Top: Irish Team
Left to Right: Owen Dempsey, Darren Duncan, Padraig Murphy, Jimmy Upton, Jonathan Lewins

Bottom: Irish Kick Boxing team
Back Row: Jonathan Lewins, Nick Russell, Reggie Byrne, Owen Dempsey, Darren Duncan, Tony McCann
Front Row: Padraig Murphy, Martin Cousins, Jimmy Upton, Michael McDermott

Figure 65. Post Tenebras Cup

Clockwise:
Martin Cousins, Jonathan Lewins, Owen Dempsey, Reggie Byrne
Owen Dempsey and Martin Cousins
Irish Team

Kenpo Karate has given me fantastic opportunities to travel and represent my country. It is good to see my pupils do so as well.

CHAPTER 6

Karate Master

My younger brother Terry was in the scouts in Dun Laoghaire. Their hall was in Patrick Street and Mick Watson and I got permission to open classes in Kenpo Karate there.

Figure 66. Scout Hall, Patrick Street, Dun Laoghaire and Ballybrack Workman's Club

However, we stopped training there after a few months because the hall was too close to the existing Kenpo club at the Workman's Club in Dun Laoghaire. Mick stayed in the Workman's Club in Dun Laoghaire and I opened a club in the Workman's club in Ballybrack village.

My wife and I had recently move to Loughlinstown and the club was only short distance from our house. Anne, my wife, and her younger brother, Michael, always known as Mick, started practising Kenpo there and when my brother Terry joined, it really became a family affair.

Figure 67. Mick Byrne, Anne Cousins and Martin Cousins

Clockwise:
Tommy Jordan and Mick Byrne
Anne Cousins and Martin Cousins sparring, Loughlinstown Leisure Centre
Mick Byrne and Martin Cousins, training in Wicklow

Anne was very good student and a good competitor, beating many male fighters.

Figure 68. Anne Cousins and Martin Cousins training, Ballybrack Workman's club, 1982

Michael became my first black belt and also won a national title in the O.N.A.K.A.I championships. Terry moved to Australia and still lives there today.

I moved my club in 1983 to Loughlinstown Leisure Centre

Figure 69. Training Places

Clockwise:
Loughlinstown Leisure Centre
Site of the Ballybrack Youth/Community Centre
St. Brendan's College, Bray
Blackrock, Co. Dublin

I also taught young students in the Ballybrack Community Centre, and classes were held for short periods in St. Brendan's College and in a hall in Blackrock.

There were many local kids who took up Kenpo in the community but only one student lasted the distance. Derek McKeever, who started in the community hall as a small six year old with all his friends, graded to black belt twelve years later when he was eighteen, becoming the youngest black belt in the history of the I.K.A.

Figure 70. Derek McKeever and Martin Cousins

There were a lot of good students emerging from the leisure centre. These included Fran Murdiff, Gerry Pluck, Liam Farrelly and Jim Maguire. Liam was a gifted competition fighter who won many trophies for the club. However, it was Fran and Gerry who would become black belts in years to come.

Figure 71. Martin Cousins sparring Liam Farrelly, Loughlinstown Leisure Centre

I had also started teaching an adult Kenpo class in Cabinteely school. This was a 10 week course under the adult education program. I taught that program for six years.

Figure 72. Cabinteely Community School and Monkstown School

In 1985 the club was on the move again. This time we started classes in Monkstown Farm in the local school.

That same year I decided to test for my 2nd Dan. Tommy Jordan agreed and I travelled to Rathgar every Friday night for a year to take a class under Tommy. Times were hard and there was a lot unemployment. Since I didn't have the luxury of a car, I had to make two bus journeys to get there, one to get into Dublin and another to Rathgar.

Figure 73. Rathgar Club Members

Left to Right: Peter Coyle, Dave Quinn, Brian O'Toole, Dick Comerford, Irene Oglesby, Tommy Jordan, Maire Ni Conaill, Richie Mahony

One of the criteria for a 2nd Dan at that time was the bow form. However, Tommy dropped it because a lot of the black belts were not learning the form. This was fortunate as I hadn't learnt it either!

Figure 74. Richie Mahony demonstrates the bow form

On the 10th of December 1987 in Monkstown school I tested for my 2nd Dan. Jimmy Rice attended as he did for my 1st Dan. My Dad and my brother Joey also attended. It was the first time my Dad had seen me doing karate. Joey had Downs Syndrome and loved to put on a karate suit. When Tommy came out to grade, he would often playfully spar with Joey.

Figure 75. Martin Cousins and Joey Cousins

Figure 76. Gaining my 2nd Dan, 1987

1988 was a bad year personally. In September my brother Hubert died after a problem developed with his heart. We had started weight training with Tony Reynolds and Liam Farrelly. We trained in Liam's shed.

Figure 77. Hubert Cousins training hard

Hubert was very interested in weights and had joined Slender Health in Stillorgan as well. He also trained in martial arts. I decided the following year to start a memorial weight lifting annual event in memory of Hubert. The first winner of the event was Tony Reynolds.

Figure 78. Tony Reynolds, first winner of the Hubert Cousins Memorial Superstars, 1989

Figure 79. Hubert Cousins Memorial Superstars, 1990s

Top: 1995, Winner Tony Devine
Centre 1994, Winner Derek McCann
Bottom:1993, Winner Martin Cousins

Other winners included Ken Earls in 1991 and Keith Nevin in 1992.

We participated in the O.N.A.K.A.I. championships again in 1989.

Figure 80. O.N.A.K.A.I. championships, 1989

Top: Mick Byrne,
Bottom: Martin Cousins and Paul Duffy

In 1989 Mick Byrne graded to black belt. Mick was my first student to get a Dan grade.

Figure 81. Mick Byrne wins a breaking competition, Top Hat, Dun Laoghaire

Figure 82. Mick Byrne gains his black belt

Clockwise:
Gerry Pluck, Mick Byrne and Martin Cousins
Mick Byrne with his sister, Anne Cousins
Mick Byrne and his father, Larry Byrne
Mick Byrne with his family, Left to Right: Cindy Reynolds, Karin Byrne, Elsie O'Gorman, Larry Byrne (Junior) Larry Byrne, Anne Cousins, Adrienne Mullen

In April 1990 two more students, Fran Murdiff and Gerry Pluck, graded to black belt.

Figure 83. Gerry Pluck, Tommy Jordan, Martin Cousins and Mick Byrne

Figure 84. Martin Cousins, Gerry Pluck and Tommy Jordan demonstrate form 6

The club competed in the O.N.A.K.A.I. championships in 1990 and again I reached the final in the individual section.

I was preparing for my 3rd Dan in December 1990, when in November my brother Joey died suddenly. My back was playing up again and I was attending the chiropractor on a regular basis. On the day of my test it went out again. Dr. Gilmore, who was my chiropractor at the time, was away on his Christmas holidays in Canada. I applied a tube of Deep Heat to my back. Tommy asked me if I wanted to cancel the grade. I refused, but looking back at the video it seems as if my mind was elsewhere.

In the I.K.A. there were some very good black belts and lower belt students emerging.

In 1992 Rathgar sent a team to Cork city to compete in the O.N.A.K.A.I. team event. Gerry Crow, Leo Williams, Craig Ennis, Willie O'Neill and Ken Keating and I were in the team. The team was narrowly beaten in the final. Ken and Willie are now instructors in Rathgar.

Figure 85. Rathgar team, O.N.A.K.A.I. championships, Cork, 1992

Figure 86. Ken Keating and Martin Cousins, I.K.A. championships

Derek McKeever had travelled with the team but was too young to compete, as it was a senior event. He was training hard for his second brown belt and he was tested in Rathgar studio later that year.

In 1992 the club moved premises again. This time we moved to St. Fintans Villas in Deansgrange. The premises were an old shed with no roof that my father-in-law had started years earlier. With the help of some of the students we built the club which is still running today. The club was great because for the first time the students could train seven days a week.

Figure 87. St. Fintans Villas

Over the years there was a lot of maintenance on the building and Gerry Pluck, Fran Murdiff, and Kevin Kane in particular worked hard on this. Without their help the club would not be here today.

Figure 88. Restoring the clubhouse at St. Fintans

Martin Cousins and Mick Byrne putting long hours into restoring the clubhouse at St Fintans

Figure 89. Kenpo Karate at St. Fintans, c.2001

Alan Ellis was still training with me and graded in 1993. He left shortly after that to train with Tommy Jordan in Rathgar. There were some good students coming through the ranks like Ross Cowap, Kevin Kane, Reg Byrne, Lar Breen, Niall McGowan and many more

Figure 90. Kevin Kane, Student of the Year, 1998

In 1994 the club help me celebrate my 40th birthday in Bakers Corner Pub in Deansgrange.

Figure 91. Celebrating my 40th Birthday, Bakers Corner Deansgrange, 1994

Derek McKeever tested for and gained his black belt in Deansgrange in 1995.

Figure 92.   Derek McKeever at his 1st Dan grading

Left to Right: Tommy Jordan, Derek McKeever and Martin Cousins after Derek's 1st Dan grading

I also tested for my 4th Dan in May that year. I was the first person in the I.K.A to be awarded the 4th Dan black belt.

Figure 93. Martin Cousins, 4th Dan

Clockwise
Receiving my 4th Dan certificate from Tommy Jordan
Martin Cousins
Jimmy Rice, Martin Cousins and Tommy Jordan at the 4th Dan grading

The problem with my back flared up again; unfortunately the damaged vertebrae could not be repaired. However my new chiropractor, Dr. Sean Wall really helped me. He had a background in sport and understood and guided patients through his work as a chiropractor. Best of all, he never told me to stop training. However, with the change in chiropractic techniques, I was getting longer spells without back pain. I can't thank him enough for care and understanding.

Figure 94. Dr. Sean Wall

Figure 95. Training at Powerscourt Waterfall, 1997

Left to Right: Reggie Byrne, Gerry Pluck, Fran Murdiff, Mick Byrne, Derek McKeever, Ross Cowap

In 1998 I left the I.K.A. and set up East Coast Martial Arts. It was a very hard decision to make, but at the time I needed a change as I was becoming disillusioned with the system I was teaching.

Reggie Byrne tested for his black belt in 1999. He was a former full-contact fighter from the kick boxing club in the old Kenpo club in Dun Laoghaire which had changed over to kick boxing. Mel Curry and then Keith Nevin, two well known full-contact fighters were in charge of the kick boxing club. Kick boxing in Dun Laoghaire had started in the old club in the 1980s. After Mel finished in traditional karate, he had taken up kick boxing which was only starting in Ireland. Mel soon became a very good full-contact fighter with many wins to his credit. He left to live in Canada and left the club in the hands of Keith Nevin who in turn became a champion himself. Sadly Mel passed away in Canada, a tragic loss for his family and also for sport.

Figure 96. Mel Curry

In 1999 we decided to bring back kick boxing to Dun Laoghaire and Reggie Byrne and I started kick boxing classes in Deansgrange. That same year we joined the All Styles Kick boxing Association of Ireland

One student at that time fighting full-contact was Owen Dempsey, who decided to join my club and practice Kenpo. Another young prospect was Jason Kane. Both were from Pottery Road and came up the ranks together.

Figure 97. Owen Dempsey and Jason Kane

Top: Martin Cousins demonstrates with Owen Dempsey
Bottom: Owen Dempsey, Martin Cousins and Jason Kane, 2000

Unfortunately, Reggie Byrne then left the club and the kick boxing stopped for a while.

Figure 98. Sparring with my son, Dean Cousins, at St. Fintans Club, 2000

In 2000 I worked with Alan Ellis again. Alan was teaching full time in Wicklow. He was now a black belt and had some very good students.

Figure 99. Martin Cousins, Alan Ellis and Alan's students

We decided to form the Irish Senior Council for grading purposes and to develop Kenpo in general. Alan arranged for Larry Tatum a 10th degree Dan from Pasadena, to give us a series of seminars in Wicklow.

Figure 100. Larry Tatum

CLockwise:
Larry Tatum and class: Left to Right: James Leonard, Ray Ellis, Alan Ellis, Reggie Byrne, Larry Tatum and Martin Cousins
Larry Tatum teaching class
Derek McKeever and Willie O'Neill at the Larry Tatum Seminar

He then organised for Francisco Soto from Mexico to do the same. It was a lot of work for Alan. I had some input, but it was Alan who brought the instructors to Ireland.

Figure 101. Francisco Soto demonstrating a technique in Wicklow

That same year I was graded to 5th Dan by the Senior Council. Subsequently the Senior Council graded Danielle Serpico to the rank of black belt.

Figure 102. Gaining my 5th Dan

Clockwise:
Martin Cousins, Alan Ellis, Danielle Serpico and Fran Murdiff
Holding the 5th Dan certificate
With my wife, Anne
With my sons, Martyn and Dean, and daughter Kaime

The last instructor Alan brought over from England was Damien Abbott who gave some seminars. A short time later I left the Senior Council.

Figure 103. Tommy Jordan, Martin Cousins and Damien Abbott

I was invited to sit on a panel of senior black belts in Rathgar for Tommy Jordan's 6th degree black belt. This grade was long over due, and I was delighted to return to the club to see some of the people I trained with and to support Tommy. He still impresses me today with his dedication and skills and is a true master.

Figure 104. Tommy Jordan's 6th Dan grading panel

In 2002 Owen Dempsey graded for his black belt.

Figure 105. Owen Dempsey's 1st. Dan grading

Left to Right: Andy O'Connor, Wesley Stephenson, Owen Dempsey, Martin Cousins, Jason Kane and Trevor Daly

After the grade, Owen started the kick boxing classes again. While teaching kick boxing he started practising Jujitsu, and became an Irish title belt holder in Ultimate Fighting. He won his belt in Belfast.

He has competed in boxing, kick boxing, grappling, Taekwon-do, and traditional karate. He has also trained in Thai boxing.

Figure 106. Owen Dempsey Belfast title fight

Clockwise:
Winning his fight in Belfast
Owen Dempsey, Irish Title Holder
Martin Cousins and Trevor Daly, Belfast
Dave Jones, Owen Dempsey's instructor, with Owen Dempsey and supporters, Belfast

He is, without doubt, the most versatile fighter I have trained, and is still fighting to the present day.

Figure 107. Dublin, Full-contact, 2001

Top: Owen Dempsey and Martin Cousins,,
Bottom: Owen Dempsey, Full-contact, Dublin 2001

In 2003 Niall McGowan approached the Grainstore community centre in Cabinteely with a view to starting class in the hall. I left Owen Dempsey in charge of Deansgrange club and I started teaching with Niall in Cabinteely. The Grainstore is the perfect place with plenty of room inside and with the park grounds to train in when the weather is good.

Figure 108. The Grainstore, Cabinteely Park

Top: The Grainstore building
Bottom: Group forms at the Grainstore
Left to Right: Niall McGowan, Laura Byrne, Martin Cousins, Adam Hennessy, Emer Lawlor and Sean Smith

In November that year I brought my students back to compete in the O.N.A.K.A.I. championships. Peter Coyle was still president and welcomed us with open arms. It had being some years since I attended a championship. We won six medals that day, with the highlight being Trevor Daly winning gold in his weight division and silver in the open weight division. It was his first time he had competed in a big tournament.

Figure 109. O.N.A.K.A.I. Championships and other tournaments, 2004

Clockwise:
Trevor Daly, Wesley Stephenson, Owen Dempsey
Laura Byrne, Emer Lawlor and Christin Fiegler, Club Tournament, St. Fintans
East Coast Martial Arts, O.N.A.K.A.I. Championships 2004 Andrew Byrne, Wesley Stephenson, Kevin Murdock, Trevor Daly, Martin Cousins, Owen Dempsey, Scott Egan, Sean Smith, Fergal Brophy, Patrick McDonagh and Chris Nicholls

Emer Lawlor was narrowly beaten in the final of the woman's open weight division and Wesley Stephenson took a bronze medal for the second year running.

I returned to Rathgar yet again to support Dave Quinn who was testing for his 3rd Dan. Dave had been very ill for some years, but never lost the will to train in Kenpo.

Figure 110. Dave Quinn receives his 3rd grade Dan

I put a program together to test for my 6th Dan. It was the hardest and most demanding grading I ever did. With the help of all my students and black belts, I achieved my goal in the summer of 2004.

Figure 111. 6th Dan, 2004

Clockwise:
Teaching class
Having a break
Sparring with Niall McGowan
With my son Dean after my 6th Dan grading. Dean was and still is my personal trainer.

Liam Whelan started training in Kenpo karate with Mel Curry. Mel and Liam were both personal friends and former members of the Dun Laoghaire Kenpo club, and had started global kick boxing with Jimmy Upton. Liam was always interested in self-defence because of his background in Kenpo. He entered the W.P.K.A. Intercontinental and European championships in Hungary and won gold and bronze medals. He also won silver medals in the World Martial Arts Peace Games in Barcelona.

Figure 112. Liam Whelan and Martin Cousins

Liam approached me in 2004 and asked me if I was interested in starting a self-defence division in A.K.A.I. The All Styles Kick boxing board agreed to let self-defence compete for the first time in its history, and that year at the national championships we produced the first winner from the East Coast Martial Arts club. This was Noel O'Connor who retained his title in 2005.

Figure 113. Noel O'Connor gains his brown belt
Left to Right: Owen Dempsey, Noel O'Connor, Martin Cousins, Niall McGowan

Figure 114. East Coast Martial Arts 2005

Clockwise:
O.N.A.K.A.I. championships 2005
East Coast light contact team, February 2005
East Cost Martial Arts light contact winners, February 2005 Left to Right: Shane Murdock (Winner) Kevin Murdock and Luke Curry (Runners Up)
Kevin Murdock, Full-contact, A.K.A.I., fight night, 2007

I also got involved in judging traditional and weapons forms and self-defence techniques. The East Coast Martial Arts club produced some national champions. These were Noel O'Connor (self-defence, light contact), Sean Smith (weapons, forms), Niall McGowan (self-defence, forms), and among the junior members, Laura Byrne (forms, weapons), Max Focca (forms) and Robert Owens (forms).

Figure 115. Robert Owens and Laura Byrne, National Champions

Owen Dempsey has produced some novice national champions in light contact kick boxing. These include Kevin Murdock, Stephen Ennis, Keith O Conner, and Luke Curry, who is Mel's son. Christin Fiegler, the semi-contact national champion has also trained there.

Figure 116. Christin Fiegler and Martin Cousins, Irish Open, 2006

Christin has now returned to her own country, Austria, but travels back to Ireland every year to compete in the Irish Open. The kick boxing club is now producing full-contact fighters and is called the Irish Red Dragon Kick Boxing Club.

Figure 117. A.K.A.I. and O.N.A.K.A.I. champions

Kevin Murdock gains a bronze medal at the A.K.A.I Open Championships, Dublin, 2004
Noel O'Connor (gold) and Niall McGowan (silver) medallists, A.K.A.I championships, self-defence, 2006
Niall McGowan, gold medal winner, A.K.A.I championships 2006
Chris Nicholls is presented with a bronze medal by Peter Coyle, President of O.N.A.K.A.I and Chief Referee,
O.N.A.K.A.I Championships, 2005

2006 brought sadness as well as success. Mick Watson, with whom I had trained from the very beginning, died.

I always believed that we should look for ways for sport to help the community. With the help of Niall McGowan and the students, we started fund raising some years ago to support the fight against cancer in Ireland.

Figure 118. Raising funds for Our Lady's Hospice, Crumlin, 2004

Left to Right: Sean Smith, Noel O'Connor, Vicky Ann, the hospice co-ordinator, and Martin Cousins

We have now established the Adrienne Mullen yearly cycle to support action on breast cancer. Adrienne is my wife's sister and a close friend of mine. Niall had lost his sister Mary to cancer a few years previously, so we both have a strong motivation to support cancer treatment and research. Over the past few years the club have cycled to Arklow each year to support Our Lady's Hospice, raising approximately 3000 - 5000 euros annually for them. We are already in training for 2007 and beyond.

Figure 119. Adrienne Mullen and Martin Cousins

Figure 120. Setting off on the sponsored cycle for St. Luke's, 2004

Left to Right: Sean Smith, Martin Cousins, Emer Lawlor, Damien Kelly, Noel O'Connor, Finn McGowan and Niall McGowan

Figure 121. Enable Ireland Corporate Run, 2005

It was good to meet people involved with other branches of martial arts.

Figure 122. Martin Cousins and Roy Baker, Irish Open, 2006

Roy Baker has been heavily involved in martial arts for a long time. He is the chief instructor to Bushido martial arts and has many World and European kick boxing titles and is without doubt the most successful Irish fighter in the history of martial arts.

Figure 123. Meeting other martial arts experts

Clockwise:
Presentation to Mick McDermott for his outstanding contribution to A.K.A.I.
Mick McDermott and Martin Cousins
At the I.M.AC stand, Dublin, 2000 Left to Right: Martin McMahon, Martin Cousins, Michael McDermott, Christina McMahon

In 2007 I was honoured to be awarded the I.M.A.C. Ambassador of Ireland award.

Figure 124. 2007 I.M.A.C. Award

Competitions continued at the National A.K.A.I. Championships in February 2007. There were several medallists.

Figure 125. Medal Winners, Monaghan 2007

Left to Right: Sean Smith, Niall McGowan, Martin Cousins (Referee) Shane McCaffrey

I believe that as martial arts instructors, we have to constantly challenge the art and ourselves to find the best ways to survive in the increasingly dangerous and ever-changing environment we live in today. People in Kenpo claim that the new system is everything. I consider that the new system is very impractical; what we learn does not work in reality. If attacks in self-defence became in any way aggressive, the techinque breaks down; techniques which are 12 or 13 moves long, even in a demonstration environment, are only practical if there is no response from your opponent.

During an attack on the street, the technique must change after the first attack and defence to survive. After the first one or two moves you must be ready to improvise and react to anything that comes your way. I introduced a cross training programme which includes kick boxing, grappling, bag work and pad work to develop strength, stamina and fitness and above all the ability to survive in real martial arts and on the street today.

That is why I will always teach my students techniques that are not deliberately complicated, but which will help them defend themselves in real life. Kenpo karate came out of street fighting; with the danger on the streets of Ireland and elsewhere today, it provides the best techniques, if taught properly, for self-defence.

I will continue to practice the sport of Kenpo Karate as long as I am able. It has given me fitness and strength. It has allowed me to travel and make friends at home and abroad. For that I will always be grateful.

My next student to grade to black belt will be Niall McGowan who has supported me for the last twenty years or more. Like all my students he has trained hard. Niall has been particularly helped by Dean Cousins in his preparations. Before this book is published he will have achieved his first degree black belt.

Index